The Sleepless Moon and Stars

OrangeBooks Publication

Smriti Nagar, Bhilai, Chhattisgarh - 490020

Website: **www.orangebooks.in**

First Edition, 2023

The Sleepless Moon and Stars

The dreams may sojourn beyond the horizon but someday, it will come to us. For now, hope is our soulmate.

Jyoti Singh

OrangeBooks Publication

www.orangebooks.in

Content

I. Art

Art, come lie down.

You have been running the whole day

From east to west, from dawn to dusk.

Your little mischiefs have kept me distracted.

Yet, you are my darling

And, you always will be.

I know, you need my time and attention

To play, to please, to justify,

To build your castle on the cloud,

To accompany the breeze over a flowing river,

To concretise you away from just fancy.

But, I'm too tired, let me sleep.

Today, you are so restless and reckless.

Ok, don't be sad and don't diminish.

I'll come right away to play

See, what we have created.

See, how magnificent is its form and colour!

See, what we can do together. It's magic and wonder.

Go, my child, go out in the world.

You are no more invisible to the eyes.

Every mother wants to see them flourish,

To touch the sky with glory and thrive.

Our journey now, has reached the summit

But you refined me and gave me wings to fly.

2. A Communion with God

It is the world of twenty first century

Full of crookery, meanness and treachery.

Question of your existence is grave,

But still people say they believe

Or they just pretend or really do.

The question is off course thrown upon you.

To come to prove this is again

A very low cost of pain.

I think you need a reason grand

To come here as your realm demand.

Not replying shows your coyness,

Why through hazards only show your presence?

Is it because you possess power?

But you too want your devotee and lover.

You love the lamb and not the tiger,

You just want us to be your follower.

I can neither pretend nor accept power

As because others' beliefs build a tower.

Why am I full of anger?

Either it is men's empty prayer

Or it is the way they pretend

To have faith on the religious trend.

Pondering on my childhood days

When my eyes looked pure and fresh.

I used to call you every hour

And you answered in my ear,

Made me happy being replied

But not for long, it can hide.

It was nothing but my heart's echo

Lately revealed with time's blow.

But now I wonder, was it true,

Was it myself or really you?

I felt either you within me

Or I am within you.

But the feeling faded as I grew,

The union broken and thoughts came new

Sometimes I muse over, am I God?

Upon my state, I thought a lot.

I possess power to life and destroy,

What more on earth, one may have joy!

In every soul, God resides,

The eternal lives partly in mortal lives.

If this innovation is really true,

Ages corruption, how can you do?

But everyone says you the only pure,

I too believe but not sure.

All these assumptions increase my rate,

Turns me back to the previous state.

3. Coffee

Coffee is not just an exotic beverage's name,

It makes me more human and I wish I had

The time-machine of Avenger's End Game

To travel in past and meet gaily humanity clad.

To discover for myself and feel those cafes'

The meeting, the culture, the aristocracy

Prevailed in the 18th century days

And inspiration would be sought with delicacy.

I wish I could take part

In their political, cultural and satirical confab,

Sipping hot coffee with art and heart

Which would be reviving and magical collab.

Very few know how it gave rise

To the plethora of intellectualism and concepts

But we still drink it for fresher eyes,

History is intoxicating with infinite hidden secrets.

4. Who Has Made Thee?

Who has made thee?

Shinning so bright on which you flee,

All full of art and colour

Throughout the fins, I wonder.

I indulge into some unknown prison

And try to find pretty evaluation.

I wonder really is it God,

Or the tiny wings, sitting upon the knot?

If it's really the tiny fairy Tink

Making right to everything

Come to me wherever you are,

Bless me too with some power,

Colour my life like the fly,

Reflecting long to the sky.

Teach me to walk and stop,

Excluding general human hope.

'Transcendence' is the word I heard,

But never tasted as the free bird.

Every step, I begin a new

But left the mark same as crew.

Nothing is new and pretty than you.

You bless me colour and make anew.

5. What a Pest I am!

What a pest I am!

The person whom I love,

Without whom my breath will be uneasy

But my nasty feelings are not with him.

I know it is crazy

But it's too much lovely.

I fear such instances

When I move in wrong paths

And later realize or

He makes me realize.

I love those freaky moments.

It's just a moment

But so passionate to out win

The honest regular life.

Will someone tell me the truth?

Exactly what I am?

Because I cannot understand myself,

But you are too mean to feed your own side

And tell me the truth.

No one can be my mirror

To show me the exact me.

I am still waiting for the one.

Every time I feel I found him,

But so small to recognize.

I think, no, I am sure

I am still waiting for you.

6. The Unknown Lover

Oh, my inner God! Bless me with power

To reveal my view in this hour.

So, this becomes the ages tale

Even in the hell, delight all pale.

One maiden sat on a rock;

Golden curls, pink lips, put on a fair robe.

Forlorn sat she, under the Oak tree

Waiting for some unknown love,

Bloomed in youthful beautiful dove,

Suffering for this painful youth,

Losing virginity is a kind of truth.

Loneliness has made her fairer,

Against her father, she has come here.

Sun is sinking beneath the earth

Red with richness, preparing for rebirth.

And the moon with silver light,

There comes the dark night.

Time has come to leave the shire.

She is the lovely Christen of Ford shire,

Precious and favourite to her father,

King Findrel is a fearful mastiff knight

Is the reason, no one came near:

Dear maiden Christen's plight.

Through some secret hollow space,

She enters her room into the castle.

Every night, she prayed no less

But this dark night different she felt.

She put off her fair robe,

Waiting for some unknown love.

Praying for the magical meet,

Lying on soft bed, she dreamt the touch

And moved in passion along the beat.

Height of sensation was so much

That it roused the God of love,

Could not resist came at once.

To pacify the beautiful, gorgeous dove

But could not appear in this one's.

He entered into a tiger's skin,

Raised his eyes and same passion withal.

He moved across the forest in darkness,

Found the way to castle in far less.

As some unknown magic drew him near

And he plunged into his room where

She lied on bed undressed so soft,

Aroused his passion even more that is oft.

He touched her waist and moving front

Felt the beating paining breast

For a mate to touch the soft.

She felt the touch was passionate

But her eyes remained unopened.

The tiger moved above everywhere,

Bit by bit her pain changed in pleasure.

Unaware of anything, she tossed about,

But eyes were closed for some magic throughout.

The tiger pained her more below

But she was happy to be low.

It was dark and the owl's bleat,

She enjoyed the very painful meet.

With every punch, she roused with pain,

Her sighful breath made him mad and faint.

Here and there, he kissed her whole night,

Bosom kept up and down in moon light.

He left her after her heart's content

And plunged into the forest straight

Before the sunrise and people rise,

He left her with where she lies.

Next morning, she woke up pleasant

But forgetting everything due to his enchant.

Every day she waits for her unknown lover,

The fading moon and Oak tree smiles at her.

7. The Supreme Creation

I wonder if man is the best creation.

Trees, I found more calming and naiver,

No regrets, no complaints, no rebellion,

Easy to adapt to what life is offering

I wonder if birds are not superior,

Free as freedom can be,

No obligation, no deadline, no enmity,

Fly high in the sky at its will

I wonder if intelligence has killed happiness,

Too much of reason, expectation and greed.

I want to turn into a tree- the giver

And resign myself into the hands of nature.

I wish I could soar in the rainbowed sky

Leaving all the earthly assets behind,

Feel my soul into me and liberate all ties

And once again descend on earth redefined

With optimism and strength,

Not to cheer the world but my own self.

They have understood the crux of life.

They fly high and descend on earth.

I am too on the verge of flying

But uncertain, if I would ever descend.

However, I will turn into a bird

And live the life of duality.

8. The 21ˢᵗ Century Princess

Everyday a princess wakes up in the morning

With content, she looks at the day shinning.

But it lasts only for some time,

Reality digs in with a loud chime.

One by one, all the chores are done.

Though, she is her own master and its fun.

The princess is still hidden in some corner.

She enjoys the noon delving deep into her nature.

But then comes the evening of the ring,

The princess psyche starts fading.

When hope is lost, life is lost.

Suicide is fearsome, thus she pays the cost.

She spends the night in dark dungeon,

Watches her whole life, weighing loss and gain.

One day comes, when she has to decide,

Break the shackles or take the passive side.

Once again, the dilemma lingers on,

That is how, the life goes on.

9. The Love We Want and We Need

I was drawn to love when I was sixteen,

Unaware of its nature, I felt it hypnotising.

It became my God, I was solely blinded,

Day and night, it had my attention undivided.

As a fool of love, I chanted its name instinctively,

I was in love wildly and irrevocably.

Who knows how far it would go on?

The very next year, he was fully gone.

It took time to come out of the quicksand,

I was chained and lost in no-man's land.

A ghost joined the institute for career,

The soul rested home bearing the pain severe.

The colours of college compelled my heart to unite,

Once again, I was one body and mind.

Who can resist the unforeseeable mighty love,

On my purple fins, again I was soaring high above.

I leapt with great faith to seek treasure,

Mindless of the fact if it would give me pleasure.

Unacquainted with my own self, again I faltered.

It wasn't God this time, so my conscience persevered.

A living being began the trek to post.

Duty is life and thus, sailed off the coast.

Few of the petals had been dropped somewhere,

The once beautiful rose will remain imperfect forever.

Life-partner is necessary for a social animal,

With two cracks in her heart, she played rational.

The union was secondary, their status was prime.

Two more pacts were lost in the meantime.

Little little branches added to the crevice,

Heart longed for impossible love to break the ice.

A sanguine senorita finally set foot in the lion's den,

She has kept a piece of her soul aside to love again.

Every day, she walked a new path of the unknown forest,

The wedding transpired devoid of any proper test.

A shocking reality surfaced with an acute thunder,

It wasn't for love but for materialistic procure.

Now what? All her hopes are gone,

The soul sank deeper and deeper in abyssal canyon.

The desires and aspirations watered since youth crumbled.

She turned into an empty vessel and her self-humbled.

She met face to face with the tangible essence of a void,

The last glimmer of light too is put off and destroyed.

But contrary to her abysmal state, she is at peace.

She lies at the bottom, nothing to lose and nothing to miss.

It's followed by contemplation as all the races have ceased,

Found a lifetime to resolve and the wisdom released.

All her life, she waited, craved for external affection.

The soul whispered in her ear- 'I am no less apt for the position.'

From the barren land, sprouted a pristine leaf of self-love,

It gilded all the cracks, electrified her heart and it's enough.

10. The Pied Piper of Amina-I

It was again a wintry night

With no joy, sorrow or light.

Peeping through the window right

On the way, searching for some sight.

Nothing happened, except the owl's voice,

Tussling of leaves, are the only choice.

Every day, she passed alone

Watching moon to whom, her pain is known.

Morning came with giving her a name,

The Queen of Radolf, but a shame.

Her father died in the fight

Is the reason of her plight.

Amina is only a winning prize,

Queen Filomina is actual bride.

He loved her with a passion's blaze

Amina's beauty could get no place.

That is the young queen's fate,

Every night is lifeless and desolate.

Though she wasn't jealous of her

Ting of light too was not there.

Watching meadows, lonely wandering,

Plucking flowers- red, blue and pink

Is the way, she is passing time,

Waiting for death or famine.

One day came a native maiden

Tried to help as much she can

"There came a charming Pied Piper

Who has delighted all the villagers.

Listening to his melodious tone

You will forget all you mourn.

He has such a lovely art

We all wanted to become his part."

Looking at the maiden's zeal,

A red current in her vein's fill

Still, she delayed to reply

Past five years, she lived shy.

Her heart cried but her lips shut,

Thinking so deep, she was about to cut.

The maiden saved and told she,

"Why do you live with uncertainty?

If you order the Pied Piper

You will be happy in his power."

She forgot her name and status,

At once, ordered for the lotus.

"My castle chamber should look heaven

With roses, lotus but no pain.

Tomorrow eve, I wish the happiest ever,

I will listen to his melodious shower.

I am still the daughter of King Wind cliff,

Who was known for her smile on lips."

Next day, she woke up fresh,

As morning dew and fair no less.

Throughout the night, tiny wings have worked

Now her cheeks glowed in pinkish shade.

Holding her gown, she moved forward

To look at the day from window upward.

Her reflection in pool caught Radolf's sight

Who is going on another fight,

At once amazed seeing the blossomed face,

But a man of duty, so left the palace.

She turned back to her golden mirror,

Sun too played his rays on her.

She was so happy for the eve,

Contemplating deep, what she would have.

At last, the maiden helped

Silken red gown was selected.

She gave blush to everything,

Such a temperament was never seen.

Lazily, the evening arrived

Looking herself in mirror, she sighed.

www.ingramcontent.com/pod-product-compliance
Lightning Source LLC
Chambersburg PA
CBHW061132160726
48006CB00036B/1885